First World War
and Army of Occupation
War Diary
France, Belgium and Germany

29 DIVISION
87 Infantry Brigade
Devonshire Regiment
5th (P.O.W.) Battalion (Territorials).
1 May 1919 - 31 October 1919

WO95/2305/3

The Naval & Military Press Ltd
www.nmarchive.com
Published in association with The National Archives

Published by

The Naval & Military Press Ltd

Unit 10 Ridgewood Industrial Park,

Uckfield, East Sussex,

TN22 5QE England

Tel: +44 (0) 1825 749494

www.naval-military-press.com

www.nmarchive.com

This diary has been reprinted in facsimile from the original. Any imperfections are inevitably reproduced and the quality may fall short of modern type and cartographic standards.

© **Crown Copyright**
Images reproduced by permission of The National Archives, London, England, 2015.

Contents

Document type	Place/Title	Date From	Date To
Heading	WO95/2305-3 1/5 Battalion Devonshire Regiment May 19-Oct 19		
Heading	Southern (Late 29th) Divn 87th Infy Bde 1/5th Bn Devon Regt May-Oct 1919 From 62 Div 185 Bde.		
Heading	5th (P Of W) Battalion Devonshire Regt. War Diary V/10 May 1919		
War Diary	Hilgen Hg. A+B Cop2 Nevenhaus, D Cov Tente C Coy	01/05/1919	20/05/1919
War Diary	Hilgen	21/05/1919	25/05/1919
War Diary	Burg	26/05/1919	31/05/1919
Miscellaneous	Headquarters, 2nd Southern Infantry Brigade.	01/06/1919	01/06/1919
War Diary	Burg West Hausen Preyers Muhle	01/06/1919	19/06/1919
War Diary	Solingen	20/06/1919	10/07/1919
War Diary	Burg Area	11/07/1919	28/07/1919
War Diary	Burscheid Area.	28/07/1919	31/07/1919
Heading	5th (P Of W) Bn. Devonshire Regt. War Diary August 1919 V-VI/1.		
War Diary	Burscheid	01/08/1919	17/08/1919
War Diary	Burscheid And Kuckenberg	18/08/1919	31/08/1919
War Diary	Burscheid	01/09/1919	30/09/1919
Heading	5th (P Of W) Bn. Devon Regt. War Diary. October 1919 V/15.		
War Diary	Burscheid	01/10/1919	04/10/1919
War Diary	Dellbruck	05/10/1919	31/10/1919

WO/95/2305/3

1/5 Battalion Devonshire Regiment

May '19 - Oct '19.

SOUTHERN (LATE 29TH) DIVN
87TH INFY BDE

1/5TH BN DEVON REGT
MAY - OCT 1919

FROM 62 DIV. 185 BDE

COPY No 1 — 2nd

24

May–Sept '19

V/10.

5TH (P OF W) BATTALION
DEVONSHIRE REGT.
WAR DIARY
MAY 1919.

WAR DIARY
or
INTELLIGENCE SUMMARY

5th (P.W.) Batt. DEVONSHIRE REGT.

Army Form C. 2118.

Place	Date	Hour	Summary of Events and Information	Remarks and references to Appendices
HILGEN. HQ, A + B Coys	1.5.19	9pm	Elementary Training of Section Commanders and return. STRENGTH Offrs 31 ORs 775	
	2.5.19	9pm	Do.	
NEUENHAUS, D Coy	3.5.19	9pm	Interior Economy	
	4.5.19	9pm	Divine Service. Major (B) (A/Col) V.L.N. PEARSON D.S.O. assumes command prmul.	
TENTE	5.5.19	9pm	Bathing + School Training.	
C Coy	6.5.19	9pm	Individual Training	
	7.5.19	9pm	Do. CO inspects D Coy on parade. Conference of Officers 1700 hours	
	8.5.19	9pm	Do.	
	9.5.19	9pm	Do. Lecture 1400 hrs. Subject: "United States of America."	
	10.5.19	9pm	Interior Economy	
	11.5.19	9pm	Divine Service.	
	12.5.19	9pm	Individual Training. Elementary musketry practices re	
	13.5.19	9pm	C.O. inspects C Coy and Transport Section on parade. Individual Training, elementary musketry practices.	
	14.5.19	9pm	Do.	
	15.5.19	9pm	Do. C.O. inspects H.Q. unit on parade.	
	16.5.19	9pm	Do.	
	17.5.19	9pm	Interior Economy. 1430 - 1900 hrs. Battn Sports meeting STRENGTH Offrs 31 ORs 773	
	18.5.19	9pm	Divine Services	
	19.5.19	9pm	Bathing. Platoon training commences	
	20.5.19	9pm	Platoon Training	

WAR DIARY or INTELLIGENCE SUMMARY

5th (P.W.) Battn. DEVONSHIRE REGT. Army Form C. 2118.

Copy No 1 — Page No 2.

Place	Date	Hour	Summary of Events and Information	Remarks and references to Appendices
HILGEN	21.5.19	9pm	Platoon training. Half Holiday. Kings francher	Apx
	22.5.19	9pm	Platoon. Training. B Cy. taking	Apx
	23.5.19	9pm	Platoon training	Apx
	24.5.19	9pm	Solemn Service. Half Holiday	Apx
	25.5.19	9pm	Divine Services	Apx
BURG	26.5.19	9pm	Battn. relieves 51st Dumfries Regt at BURG and is disposed as follows: HQ and C Cy. The Schloss, BURG. B Cy UNTERBURG. A Cy FREYERSMUHLE and park. D Cy WESTHAUSEN and park. Relief complete 1500 hrs.	Apx
	27.5.19	9pm	Re-organisation of posts, tricks &c.	Apx
	28.5.19	9pm	Platoon training. Musketry. Outposts &c. Outpost Cy carrying out programme as per schedule. Educated find march 0830-0930 hrs. Half Holiday	Apx
	29.5.19	9pm	Platoon training. Musketry and Outposts	Apx
	30.5.19	9pm	B & C Cys march to FREYERS MUHLE. Take left training. Inspection given en route in march discipline, advanced Guard, musketry	Apx
	31.5.19	9pm	Interior Economy. Half Holiday	Apx

STRENGTH Offrs 39 O.Rs 1119

(signed) H.P. Earle??
Comdg. 5th (P.W.) Battn. Devonshire Regt.

Headquarters,
    2nd Southern Infantry Brigade.
****

No. 3783
29 JUN 1919

Herewith War Diary of this Unit
for month of June 1919.

SOLINGEN
1st July 1919.

Lieut.Colonel.
Commanding 5th Devonshire Regiment.

WAR DIARY 5 (TOW) BATH DEVONSHIRE R (Army Form C. 2118.)
or
INTELLIGENCE SUMMARY. VOL V Cpy No I Page No 1

Place	Date	Hour	Summary of Events and Information	Remarks and references to Appendices
BURG	1-6-19	9pm	Divine Service. Strength officers 36 O.R.s 646.	
WERMESKIRCHEN	2-6-19	9/am	Working parties. Wermeskirchen and Unterburg	
FREYERSMUHLE	3-6-19	9/am	15th Coys training in advanced rear guards, outposts, posts & cov. training and musketry	
	4-6-19	9/am	Do	
	5-6-19	7pm	Do	
	6-6-19	9/am	Leave party's arrival to England	
	7-6-19	9/am	training as for 5th June	
	8-6-19	9/am	Divine Service	
	9-6-19	9/am	Divine Service	
	10-6-19	9/am	A.L.I. and Norwegians & 14 Fusiliers. A Cry and Prayers Mules, Cypes	
			Selected Bdg move Day at Westhausen	
	11-6-19	9/am	Cliff football and retro above Wulfshofen etc	
	12-6-19	9/am	Do. xxxxxxxxx and attributing Bay 4 xxxxxxxxxxxx	
	13-6-19	9/am	Do	
	14-6-19	9/am	Do	
	15-6-19	9/am	Colonel present to 5th Devon Shire Regt at Werkham by H.R.H. Duchess of Water, Colonel in chief.	
	15-6-19	9/am	Divine Service	

Army Form C. 2118.

WAR DIARY
or
INTELLIGENCE SUMMARY
(Erase heading not required.)

5 (P.O.W) Bn Devonshire Regt.
Vol V. Copy No 1. Page I

Place	Date	Hour	Summary of Events and Information	Remarks and references to Appendices
BURG	16.6.19	0930	Platoon Training (Drill, advance (Rear Guards) Company Cmdrs. Conference.	N.I.9
WESTHAUSEN	17.6.19	0900	Outpost Scheme for all Companies.	N.I.9
PREYERSMUHLE	18.6.19	0900	Outpost Companies relieved by 5/2 Bn Hampshire Regt and were billeted for night at UNTERBURG. All surplus kit & baggage sent to dump at HILGEN. Remnts to Div. Dump at MULHEIM.	N.I.9
SOLINGEN	19.6.19	0930	Battalion moved to SOLINGEN. In fighting order ready for action.	N.I.9
	20.6.19	0900	Commanding Officers Inspection of all Coys & Transport.	N.I.9
	21.6.19	0900	Gas Drill, Rifle Drill, Arms Drill, including drill, Musketry, L.G. sections L.G. drill.	N.I.9
	22.6.19	1115	Divine Service	N.I.9
	23.6.19	0930	Battalion Route March.	N.I.9
	24.6.19	0900	Bathing and Kit Inspections etc.	N.I.9
	25.6.19	0900	Gas drill, arms drill, Musketry, L.G. sections L.G. drill. Lectures by O.C. Companies Interior Economy.	N.I.9
	26.6.19	0900	do. do. do. Lectures on Guards + Sentries duties	N.I.9
	27.6.19	0900	Interior Economy.	N.I.9
	28.6.19	0900	Saluting Drill, Companies under Company Commanders, Interior Economy.	N.I.9
	29.6.19	1000	Divine Service.	N.I.9
	30.6.19	0900	Inspection of Gas Helmets. Took Demonstration at BRUHL without Battalion. Batt. Strength Offs 35 O.R. 693	N.I.9

A. Faison
Lt. Col.
Comdg 5th (P.O.W) Bn Devonsh te Regt.

WAR DIARY or INTELLIGENCE SUMMARY

Army Form C. 2118.

5th (P. of W.) Batt DEVONSHIRE Regt.
Copy No. 1 Page No. 1

Place	Date	Hour	Summary of Events and Information	Remarks and references to Appendices
SOLINGEN	1-7-19	0904	The Battalion moves to BURG AREA and is disposed as follows: Hdqrs & "D" Coy SCHLOSS BURG. A, B & C Coys billet in UNTERBURG	M.P.S.
	2-7-19	0900	Organization of Billets for Hdqrs & "D" Coy. A, B & C Coys relieve 5 Lst Hants on Outpost Line. Right Sector A Coy, Centre do C Coy, Left do B Coy. Relieving A Coy 5th (?) do C Coy do B Coy	M.P.S. M.P.S. M.P.S.
	3-7-19	0900	Education (2 hrs) Bathing, P.T. Drill	M.P.S.
	4-7-19		Holiday for all men of II Corps in Celebration of Signing of Peace Treaty. Sports & Games organized.	M.P.S.
	5-7-19	0900	Education (2 hrs) Lecture Economy	M.P.S.
	6-7-19	1000	Divine Service	M.P.S.
	7-7-19	0900	Bathing, Education, Gas Drill, P.T. 2 L.O.T.R. Oxford 2/Lt S. Matthew 6 O.R. with Colours left unit to proceed to PARIS Visit by Belle Camee	M.P.S. M.P.S.
	8-7-19	0900	Tactical Training (Outposts)	M.P.S.
	9-7-19	0900	Education (2 hrs) Musketry P.T. Gas Drill (Chaplain of Hospitals of Düsseldorf)	M.P.S.
	10-7-19	0900	Tactical Training (Practice Attack) Bathing in afternoon	M.P.S.

Army Form C. 2118.

WAR DIARY
or
INTELLIGENCE SUMMARY

(Erase heading not required.)

5th (P. of W.) Batt.
DEVONSHIRE Regt.
1 Copy No. 1. Page No. 2

Place	Date	Hour	Summary of Events and Information	Remarks and references to Appendices
BURG AREA	11-7-19	0900	Education, Wet Day Programme (Musketry & Lectures)	W.T.J.
	12-7-19	0900	Education, Interior Economy. Officers Race (100) to Cologne Races	W.T.J.
	13-7-19	0900	Divine Service	W.T.J.
	14-7-19	0830	Educational Examination for 2nd & 3rd Class Certificates of Army Education - Colour Party & Colours take part in VICTORY MARCH through PARIS.-	W.T.J. W.T.J.
	15-7-19	0830	This P.T. Geo Brig. H.Q. Instruction to for 145 wks. (Remaining nws of Companies)	W.T.J.
	16-7-19	0900	Tactical Training. 'D' Coy holding BURG DEFENCE LINE and are attached by 'C' Coy. 'A' Coy. Defence of Outpost line with counter-attack. 'B' Coy. as for 'A' Coy.	W.T.J.
	17-7-19	0900	2 hrs Education. Arms Drill, Musketry, P.T. Bathing.	W.T.J.
	18-7-19	0900	Tactical Training Scheme. Return of Colour Party & Colours	W.T.J.
	19-7-19		Holiday for all Ranks. Peace Celebration. Sports & Games.	W.T.J.
			2/Lt. F.W. Whittam 2/m O.R.returns with rations party & Colours time to Divine Service A/m O.Rs. 'D' Coy. Joined with 513 Batt. Runners Yeo. A & C Coys. Spared of 52 of Capt. Mayor & L.A.	
	20-7-19	0930		
		1130		To Brussels to take part in Victory March	

2449 Wt. W14957/Mg0 750,000 1/16 J.B.C. & A. Forms/C.2118/12.

Army Form C. 2118.

WAR DIARY
or
INTELLIGENCE SUMMARY
(Erase heading not required.)

5th (P. of W) Batt. DEVONSHIRE Rgt.
Copy No. 1. Page No. 3.

Instructions regarding War Diaries and Intelligence Summaries are contained in F. S. Regs., Part II. and the Staff Manual respectively. Title Pages will be prepared in manuscript.

Place	Date	Hour	Summary of Events and Information	Remarks and references to Appendices
BURG AREA	21-7-19	0900	Education, Musketry, P.T. Gas Drill, Bathing.	M.F.
	22-7-19	0900	Tactical Training. (Defence Exercise) - Reconnaissance of ground -) SALAMANCA DAY. - Sports in afternoon followed in the evening by a search expedition through BRUSSEL's take part in Wet Wear Programme (Education, P.T. Musketry, Lecturing on)	M.F. M.F.
	23-7-19	0900		M.F.
	24-7-19	0900	Tactical Training (Manning Outposts hrs. Night Operation (Carrying out of Batt. Defence Scheme.) Colours Party reported	M.F.
	25-7-19	0900	Gas Drill Musketry, P.T. Intelligence Economy.	M.F.
	26-7-19	0900	EDUCATION, Divine Economy	M.F.
	27-7-19	0730	Divine Service	M.F.
	28-7-19	0900	Outpost Line relieved by 52nd Devons. Batt. moves to BURSCHEID Headqrs Bn. A.B.C. Coys billeted in BURSCHEID. D Coy KUCHENBERG	M.F.
BURSCHEID AREA	29-7-19	0900	Re-organization of Billets	M.F.
	30-7-19	0900	Education, Intelligence Economy, Drill, Musketry.	M.F.
	31-7-19		(Lecturing Strong Points). Infantry Coy. to 75th Battn	M.F.

COPY No 1.

5ᵀᴴ (P ᴼᶠ W) BN. DEVONSHIRE REGT.

WAR DIARY.

AUGUST. 1919.

V - VI. / I.

WAR DIARY

5th (P.of W.) Bn Devonshire Regt Army Form C. 2118.

INTELLIGENCE SUMMARY. Vol V-VI

Copy No. 1 Page 1.

Place	Date	Hour	Summary of Events and Information	Remarks and references to Appendices
BURSCHEID	Aug 1.	9pm	Batt. with HQ at BURSCHEID, GERMANY. D Coy at KUCKENBERG. Strength Officers 38 O.Rs 831	Ynr
	2.	9pm	Company training. Rear Guard operations in mufti & wire repelling attack.	Ynr
	3	9pm	Education, Interior Economy, Musketry, Bathing.	Ynr
		9pm	Divine Service C/E, R.C., Nonconformists.	Ynr
	4.	9pm	Company Training. Obstacles. 1 Coy in Attack 2 Coys in search.	Ynr
	5.	9pm	Education, Interior Economy, Musketry, Bathing	Ynr
	6.	9pm	Lecture — Exercise for all Officers and N.C.Os.	Ynr
			Education Examination.	
	7.	9pm	Education Examination, Interior Economy, Musketry, Gas Training, Bathing, Sports & Schemes	Ynr
	8.	9pm	Interior Economy.	Ynr
			Sports. Bn Tournament, KALK, COLOGNE.	
	9.	9pm	Interior Economy	Ynr
			2nd Rd Bn Tournament. Both wins. Sports 1 first 3 thirds. Sports 1 first 2 seconds and 2 or 3 thirds	
			Transport 1 first 3 thirds	
	10	9pm	Divine Services, C/E, R.C.	Ynr
	11	9pm	3rd Day Company Training. Rear guard attacked.	Ynr
	12.	9pm	Education, Musketry, Bathing	Ynr
	13	9pm	4th Day Company Training Bomb attack. Lectures at H.Q.	Ynr
	14	9pm	Education, Infantry training, Musketry, Bathing from 1200 hours	Ynr
	15	9pm	5th Day Company Training. Consolidated defensive position is attacked.	Ynr
	16	9pm	Education, Interior Economy, Musketry	Ynr
	17	9pm	Divine Services. C/E, R.C, Nonconformists.	Ynr

WAR DIARY 5th (HOW) BN. DEVONSHIRE REGT Army Form C. 2118.
or
INTELLIGENCE SUMMARY. VOL V-VI COPY No. 1. PAGE 2.

Place	Date	Hour	Summary of Events and Information	Remarks and references to Appendices
BURSCHEID	Aug 18.	9 pm	5th Day Company Training. Coordinance Reference Parker 1/2 Marked.	9 mins
AND	19.	9 pm	Education. Interior Economy, Musketry, Bathing.	9 mins
WICKENBERG			Army Council visits three Army men passing through Burscheid en route.	
	20	9 pm	Interior Economy. A Coy on march. Interplaton Musketry Competition.	9 mins
	21	9 pm	Education. Interior Economy, Musketry, Gas Training.	9 mins
	22	9 pm	4th Day Company Training. Both Abandon consolidated positions.	9 mins
	23	9 pm	Education. Interior Economy, Musketry	9 mins
	24	9 pm	Divine Services C/E, R.C.	9 mins
	25	9 pm	Company Training. Bomb scheme carried out by Coys.	9 mins
	26	9 pm	Education. Interior Economy, Musketry	9 mins
	27	9 pm	3rd Day Company Training. Rear guard attack.	9 mins
	28	9 pm	Education. Interior Economy, Musketry	9 mins
	29	9 pm	1st Day Company Training. Advanced Guard.	9 mins
	30	9 pm	Education. Interior Economy.	9 mins
	31	9 pm	Divine Services. C/E., R.C., Nonconformist.	9 mins

Strength. 35 Officers. 792 ORs.

H. Lawson
Lt.-Col.
Comdg. 5th (P.O.W) Bttn. Devonshire Regt.

WAR DIARY 8th (P.O.W.) Bn DEVONSHIRE, REGT
INTELLIGENCE SUMMARY
Copy No 3, Page 1

Army Form C. 2118.

Instructions regarding War Diaries and Intelligence Summaries are contained in F.S. Regs., Part II. and the Staff Manual respectively. Title pages will be prepared in manuscript.

(Erase heading not required.)

Place	Date	Hour	Summary of Events and Information	Remarks and references to Appendices
BURSCHEID	Sept 1	9am	Battalion billeted at Burscheid. Germans, D Company at Kuckenberg. Strength Officers 35. O.R. 810	8HQ
	2	9am	Training. Interior Economy. Musketry. Bathing. "A" Coy throwing Aunno Grenades.	8HQ
	3	9am	Training. Outpost scheme. Outpost Coy drawn rear guard to the Battn and is attacked, attack carried out by 2 Platoons, remainder Coy Outp	8HQ
	4	9am	Interior Economy. Musketry.	8HQ
	5	9am	Inspection by Comdg Officer Band and drums, into Platoon Competition. Education Musketry.	8HQ
	6	9am	Battn parade in chars opp house Comd will intervening Colonna is 13 Gtr.	8HQ
	7	9am	Interior Economy. Musketry & Bathing. B Coy to Athens during, G & Battalion Sports	8HQ
	8	9am	Divine Service. C of E. R.C. Nonconformist.	8HQ
	9	9am	Education. Bayonet fighting. Musketry.	8HQ
	10	9am	A & C Coy selected practice in 30 yds Range Lewis Guns, & Rapid loading with Ball Ammunition. Gtr.	8HQ
	11	9am	Education. D Coy throw down Grenades, Bayonet fighting. Musketry.	8HQ
		9am	A & C Coy Company movements by Platoons Comps given them by C Coy rapid deployments, the action & control	8HQ
		9am	"D" Coy Throwing Live Grenade "B" Coy on duty. Bathing	8HQ
	12	9am	Education "A" Coy Bayonet fighting, Remainder Interior Economy	8HQ
	13	9am	Interior Economy Musketry	8HQ
	14	9am	Divine Service C of E. R.C. Nonconformists.	8HQ
	15	9am	Education. "C" Coy throwing Aunno Grenades. Remainder Musketry	8HQ
	16	9am	"C" Coy throwing Live Grenades. Remainder Bayonet fighting.	8HQ
	17	9am	Education, Bayonet fighting. Musketry.	8HQ
	18	9am	Interior Economy. Musketry. Bayonet fighting.	8HQ
	19	9am	Bayonet fighting. Musketry.	8HQ
	20	9am	Interior Economy. "D" Coy move from Kuckenberg to BURSCHEID.	8HQ
	21	9am	Divine Service. C of E. R.C. Nonconformist.	8HQ

WAR DIARY
INTELLIGENCE SUMMARY. 3rd (P.O.W.) Bn Hampshire Regt.

Army Form C. 2118.

Order N° 3 Page 11

Place	Date	Hour	Summary of Events and Information	Remarks and references to Appendices
BULFORD	Apr 22	9 am	Education, Bayonet fighting, musketry	See
	23	9 am	Battn in for Battn schemes Bayonet fighting & musketry	Sept.
	24	9 am	Bayonet fighting, musketry	"
	25	9 am	R.E. Lecture to Officers	"
	26	9 am	Officers Class, Bayonet fighting, Platoon training under Coy Comdt & Bayonet fighting	"
	27	9 am	Interior Economy, R.E. Sports	"
	28	9 am	Divisional Service, R.C. Memorial Service	"
	29	9 am	Education "D" Coy Musketry. All types Bayonet fighting assaulting musketry	"
	30	9 am	Bayonet fighting, musketry, interior Economy, salute Battn Transport Inspected Competition	"
			Strength Officers 33 O.R. 808.	Sept.

A.J. Fisher

COPY Nº 3.

5ᵀᴴ (P OF W) BN. DEVON REGT.
WAR DIARY.
OCTOBER 1914

V/15.

WAR DIARY or INTELLIGENCE SUMMARY

Army Form C. 2118.

Unit: 5" (POW) Bn 7own Regt. 334th HQ 6.O.R.

Place	Date	Hour	Summary of Events and Information	Remarks and references to Appendices
BURSCHEID	1st	9 am	Education & Lewis machtry	SHR Capt
"	2	9 am	Kitchenel Transport turnout, Competition, Coy. Interior economy.	SHR Capt
"	3	9 am	Education, musketry & bayonet fighting	SHR Capt
"	4	9 am	Battn moves in march route to DELLBRUCK.	SHR Capt
"	5	9 am	Division service & F.E. R.C. Wulveran.	SHR Capt
DELLBRUCK	6	9 am	Divine service	SHR Capt
"	7	9 am	Lewis Gunner visited Ranges all Officers & MG's	SHR Capt
"	8	9 am	Result of Transport turnout No 88 print Commers Lining Fault I Practise I II III IV	SHR Capt
"	9	9 am	Battn Firing Part II Practices V VI VII Annual Course	SHR Capt
"	10	9 am	Battn Firing Part II Practices 8 & 9.	SHR Capt
"	11	9 am	Battn Firing Part II Practise 10,11 & 12. ARA Platoon Competition at Funk 110	SHR Capt
"	12	9 am	Battn Firing Part II Practise 10, 11 & 12 to finish	SHR Capt
"	13	9 am	Lewis Service by F.E. R.C. Wulveran. Result of Turnout & Drill Competition 7½/63	SHR Capt
"	14	9 am	Annual Course musketry Part II Practises No 13 & 14	SHR Capt
"	15	9 am	Annual Course musketry Part II Practises 15 & 16.	SHR Capt
"	16	9 am	Annual Course musketry Part III Practises 17,9,18	SHR Capt
"	17	9 am	Annual Course musketry Park II Practise 19. October	SHR Capt
"	18	9 am	Interior Economy. Clothing & Equipment Inspection.	SHR Capt
"	19	9 am	Divine Service by F.E. R.C. Wulveran. Kits Inspection Interior Economy	SHR Capt
"	20	9 am	Names sent in of R.C. Wulveran.	SHR Capt
"	21	9 am	Baths for Battn P.O.W. Camp hullBruck. Officer Strength	SHR Capt
"	22	9 am	150 NCO & men to 31st Bn huts Regt B Cay G (POW) Camp DELLBRUCK.	SHR Capt
"	23	9 am	Commenced storing Lewis gun Educational Equipment. MULHEIM. 3rd Class sub steam	SHR Capt
"	24	9 am	Storing of Equipment. MULHEIM. 14 Officers 273 OR 16 52 horses 8 b/r 16 51 horses	SHR Capt
"	25	9 am	Co of us G transport Linbus landed in MULHEIM. All NCO & Men cleaning up Billets	SHR Capt

Army Form C. 2118.

WAR DIARY
or
INTELLIGENCE SUMMARY.
(Erase heading not required.)   5 P. of W. DEVON. REGT.

Instructions regarding War Diaries and Intelligence Summaries are contained in F.S. Regs., Part II. and the Staff Manual respectively. Title pages will be prepared in manuscript.

Place	Date	Hour	Summary of Events and Information	Remarks and references to Appendices
DELLBRÜCK	Oct 26	9 pm	Move to MÜHLEM	
	27	9 pm	Handed in 33 mules to Div. Train. 3 Riders to 2/5 How.ry Bde	S/17
	28	9 am	Transport them sent to the 52nd heavy Artillery Equipment handed in to OR.D.O.S	S/17
	29	9 pm	Investigation Stores Clerical Receipt for same	S/17
	30	9 pm	Spent Jour Ratines. Field trainings. all fit under Blethine & Ammunition to Relieve	S/17
	31	9 pm	Finished packing up. Crew two for Greno. Strength 9 Officers 37 O. Ranks	S/17

attached to 5th Hosps 1 Officer 4 O. Ranks.
—"— 82 train 1 O. Rank.
—"— Advanced Rhine Army 5 O. Ranks.

V. G. Easton
Lieut. Colonel.
Comdg. 5th (P. of W.) Devonshire Regt.

www.ingramcontent.com/pod-product-compliance
Lightning Source LLC
Chambersburg PA
CBHW081509160426
43193CB00014B/2629